ISBN-13: **978-1-7321319-3-4**

Written by: LaShonda C. Henderson
Published by: Cshantay Publishing

Copyright 2018

Why I can't go to the Altar

~For Love and Community, may we find our way

Al·tar

a usually raised structure or place on which sacrifices are offered or incense is burned in worship *—often used figuratively to describe a thing given great or undue precedence or value especially at the cost of something else*

a table or place which serves as a center of worship or ritual

~Merriam Webster's Dictionary 2018

Hi, it is me, Selah, and I am back with another set of stories. While the other stories I shared were specifically about love, this time, I am acting as an intercessory. Some of you know what it is, but some are asking, what exactly is that?

I will make no assumptions and will tell you the only way I know how....

You see, where I am from, deep in the South, we worship wherever we can. Sometimes it is in a house, it might be in a yard, storefront or even in a big beautiful building brought by the community building fund, collected by the tithes of the people who live there. But one thing they all have in common, is that they are called, the house of worship. In those sacred places, we have unwritten rules about sharing our hearts with one another. If it is a good trustworthy spot, exempt from the holy gossip ghost, you will find people telling all their troubles to people they would hardly ever encounter.

Yet, the rule within the communities about prayer, for people in distress, is; having someone else pray for you is way more powerful than praying alone. Because of this, we isolate and turn to specific ones to pray. In some cultures, we would have called them seers, or shamans; but in this day and time, we have a different name we call them, those words will come later, right now let me tell you about them before we talk about why we call them what we do.

We do it because we feel these people are appointed to pray, they have seen life, and they can envision success for your petition when you feel you do not have the words or know what steps to take forward when you are in a hard place.

They can be a gentle soul or what appears to be a harsh seasoned person of the community; depending on their life walk. Usually, they have deep wrinkles and hearts that have beat for many situations; yet, they have overcome. Yes, we call them "PRAYER WARRIORS" because they have seen many battles, spiritual and flesh/physical ones.

You do not have to know who they are, for they are called to their prayer space by leaders or pastors.

But for some, we find them through people who know them and share their power by word of mouth. In the "streets" as we say, they are the house where people go to for love and comfort, they are often a phone call away.

But in the temples, they stand up with grandeur or humbleness, depending on the type of person they are; called forward by a shout, song, or simple request sent vibrating throughout the gathering.

Whatever method used, this call, signals the prayer warriors to move to the front of the body of worshipers. There is usually a hush that follows and the sound echoes throughout the building, "If you need prayer come to the arms waiting to speak on your behalf." "Come to the Altar."

The congregation sits with breath held and eyes following the ones bold enough to step up and ask a seasoned prayer warrior for assistance. Before a word is uttered, they reach out to touch the requestor; and for some, this is the only touch they have had all day, week, or month. The warrior then begins by asking what is it that you want prayer for and the intercessory begins.

Now please do not get me wrong and think that I am saying that I think I am the church or even on the same level as those warriors. I make no claims about that. I am just a woman, one who listens and keeps secrets.

Well, life is the church and we all need prayer at one time or another. But I send no petitions forward, I sit quietly while a person tells their story, then speak out loud for both our hearts to be cleared of the burden they speak. But really, you can call it prayer.

Oh, I do pray; and when they leave, I pray alone for me too. I pray that I have a heart that is open and ears that will listen and a mouth that stays shut against the secrets that lead people to believe life has taken them down a path where prayer becomes an urgency, so pressing that it keeps them from walking into the body of worshippers. You see, people in those bodies pray for normal things.

But the people who come to me, say things that would not be deemed appropriate, for they are questing the very existence or need of the body. I did not determine that, they did. Shhhhh, I hear someone coming now, listen…

"Daddy"

Selah, I cannot go to the Altar because my Father died on the side of a busy street; and no one knew who he was.

And you know the strange thing is, that he barely knew who I was.

You know, I did not even make it to his funeral. But I remembered the start of it all, so fresh in my mind; that the phone still rings from time to time, much like when he was alive. Let me tell you how it was.

I can hear the ringing of the phone, and when it began to blast, I walked over to it in a hurry, because Selah, I knew it was him calling me. But, that last call, was weird, you see it had been like a couple of weeks since I last spoke to him and this was the relief I was waiting for, to hear his voice; you see, no one called this line but him.

But, instead of his voice; it was another familiar voice. The sound of his brother's came booming through the line, insinuating that I did not care. That I should be there with everyone. He said, "your Father was just found laying on the street, in the hospital under John Doe and you are not even trying to make it here."

But I did care.

I wanted to get there fast enough, but the room was spinning so slowly and my bank account, its emptiness caused it to spin even slower. I did care, but he was right, I could not get there fast enough.

But I tried Selah, I promise I did. But I could not get a loan to get to him and my paycheck was not nearly enough to get us there; my baby, my brother, and I. I sat in that moment and promised I would be rich someday, so I would never have to worry about what to do next. You see even though he did not feel responsible for me. I felt responsible for him.

I mean all I had was this image of him that I clung to inside my head; a picture so clear of a strong black man, you know the kind who picks up his daughter and kisses her face for no good reason? One whose arms are so strong that he could hold the world up? I know it sounds poetic and story like; but Selah, that is really what I thought; it was all I had when I did not have him.

I saw all the faces of kids, teenagers and grown women like me, being held by arms that seemed like that poetic thought, so I know it existed and it helped me see, that I was not asking for too much.

I mean, looking at them it felt that way to me; like it was me that was meant to be in arms like that. You know, a slow frozen frame of love, like you see in the movies? One of those black and white ones that appeared on the television at home, except those characters were white, but with my imagination, I made it possible that he could be black. That the man on the screen could be a man I knew, my Father treating ME in that way.

Eventually, when the money came, I hopped on that plane, chasing that accusatory voice flowing in my head, "You'd think you don't care."

But Selah, do you know how much a daughter needs her father? Do you know that sometimes her desire for him intermingles into the idea of what GOD is supposed to be? Not on purpose though. It is never on purpose, just a happenstance that cannot be avoided. Except instead of Jesus as a savior, Daddy is; and instead of an inanimate object hung on a cross, the image comes alive and manifest into a man. Except he got down long before I could see him and was out there in the world saving other people's daughters. Saving daughters when he should be saving his own. A regular ordinary man who shows up for his son and rolls his eyes at his daughter.

He died alone and maybe he was on his knees praying for forgiveness asking for someone, anyone to save him. And maybe it was another man he asked, one stronger than he was when HE did not save me. I cannot go to the Altar because I am still a little angry at GOD and I know he sees my heart.

So, can you pray for me?

The Exchange

I hear your story. I want to say, Sis, I am so sorry you had those things happen. But I want to say this, and I am not taking anything away from your experience, but hear me out:

Nothing you did or could have done could have changed the way your

Father saw you. No dance you could perform, no special ability or action could change him.

Who he was, belonged to him.

His choices

His behavior

His idea of love

His needs

All belonged to him. Now I know you feel hurt and are overflowing with the what ifs and maybes. But what happened, can not be changed. He can never go back and be the Father you needed him to be. But YOU get to decide the type of person you will be going forward.

No matter what you think.

GOD, the Almighty, the MOST HIGH, the GREAT IAM is not the personification of your Father. You must separate the two if you want to survive. Because if you do not, you will find yourself alone. Not alone in the physical, but alone in the choices you make. Whatever you believe of GOD, muster it together; embrace the feeling of comfort you feel when something goes right. Because Sis, something is right, you are here before me, asking for a return to the deep part of yourself. Because while your Father was a power in your life outside of you, GOD is in you. And to believe that you cannot reach that power is to believe that you cannot reach yourself. Do you understand that?

No matter what happens out there in the world, that unpredictable place; know that what happens in you is predictable. You are in control of that. Know that, how you feel about you, is how you will engage that world out there.

Repeat after me: "Prayer is me talking to GOD and my actions are my acceptance or rejection of the answers given to me."

Sis, let us bow our head and hear the words as they come from wherever it is that GOD lives.

The Prayer

Great IAM, we know very little about life, we have no answers; and we know even less about the actions of other people. But in this moment, we come to you with no assumptions about what others are. We come with no assumptions nor requirements on what they should be. We know our past and understand that despite any obstacles we had to overcome, we are here in the NOW. And now is where progress happens. We ask humbly for you to remove the weight of performance of our hearts. Help us to understand that we are only responsible for ourselves. That peace can only begin when we give ourselves and others a blank slate. Reset our minds to allow other people to be the perfectly flawed beings and still love them. For we know not the effort it takes, for ANYone to walk this earth. May you find the space for us to forgive ourselves for not being the picture we created in our minds. Help us to focus on daily progress, instead of what we did not become or do. Stand with us as we perform the daily walk of tearing down the monuments we built of people and ourselves. For we are all human. Walk with us in our decisions and guide us towards a new mind.

Amen, which means we stand in agreement.

Sis, now you do the work. Let go, one idea at a time; not of your Father, but the pain of who he could not be for you.

I love you.

Wipe your tears.

You did nothing wrong.

I will pray with you any time, but you have the power to pray too. I need you to understand that you should not place anyone else on a pedestal, me included. I am just a person and I will make mistakes so do not look for holiness from me. Let nothing I do hinder your relationship; for prayer is simply your personal conversation with the Most HIGH and it is not the messenger that has power, but the requester.

But what if I pray wrong; or GOD is busy, what if GOD cannot hear me?

Sis, whatever you say honestly from your heart is prayer, words or not. If you need me, I am here, but you must feel your way towards the Altar yourself. But should you call me to stand beside you, until you gain confidence, I am here, I may come flawed, but I will be there.

"Community"

I am not a racist

I am a humanist

But it is the people who look like me, who are denied their HUMAN-ness in front of my eyes; Daily.

The fact that I celebrate the denial of a large part of this community, and it causes them to get irritated; is not my problem. It is their problem, one that lives in THEM, that supports the chaos out there. There is no justice for us.

Selah, why should I go to the Altar, when no one sees me. They gave us this GOD and if I do not exist to them, how on earth can I matter to their most sacred judge, when even the knowledge of the essence was a gift?

I am not talking foolish, I see the look on your face.

This is far from blasphemous, I know exactly what the history books say. You see, their GOD came from somewhere before they gave it over to us. Tell me where did GOD come from? They made this "HIM" up. I got the videos, books, and time to prove it. But even with everything I know, this GOD is all I have, and no matter the origin, I seek to be acknowledged. This is the ONE I come back to when I am afraid or confused, and right now, I do not know which way to turn.

If I told you the joy that came into my life, after entering the Sanctuary for the first time you would not believe me.

Inside those walls, hope felt like a person, sitting in the back row, like a guest Pastor waiting for their chance to come to the mic. And me, I walked right in and sat up front. My eyes glowed with wonder as people touched one another. My mouth drooled with want when people ran up and down the aisle filled with the spirit.

I decided that the front would be my position after I saw that, just in case any spirit fell off anyone, I wanted to be the one to pick it up. Should I catch any, I wanted to place it in a jar, or rub it all over me and add it to my own spirit for protection, for it felt like life!

The best part was when the Pastor would get up and preach directly to me. I know the building was filled with people from all walks of life and situations, but he contacted me. Somehow, maybe he peeked into my window or saw me on the street, I don't know, but it felt like every word said, fit my situation.

It did not matter that I had this deep dark skin or coarse frazzled hair; the message was no respecter of persons, and it talked to ME using Pastor's voice as the vehicle. I was there for every single service. Sunday, Bible study, Men's church, Saturday social gatherings, usher boards; if the building was open, I was there.

At every event I was elated, "Full of the Spirit" they call it. Among all this feel-good notion, I was called to order when I stood up one Sunday and said I wanted to be a member. The body of people clapped and cheered like they were happy they won me over.

But right away, I was placed into this new believer's class. I was ecstatic because this was the induction that made me one of them fully! I was sure that they would tell me the secrets to catch the real holy spirit and how to pray properly, you know things like that.

I went to the class and sat near the Deacon and Deaconess; pen, paper, and bible in hand. I was ready Selah! I was going to take copious notes and write down all the tips I needed to become a good member. But the class was not about learning spiritual things, it was more about what they called, "decency and order." The rules of acting, the reasons why they believed, how to have faith.

But I thought this was my chance. You know, the opportunity for the Elders to tell me exactly what this GOD is and how I could gain attention to get loved too. Because they kept telling me in the sermons that GOD was pure love and I needed some of that in my life.

But I was not allowed to ask those types of questions. As intellectual as I am, they wanted me to sit back and be told what GOD is, with no input on how I felt or how I could get close. They made the MOST HIGH into this slave master who only wanted me to follow rules without question and have "faith" as they said. I sat solemn, wondering if I was supposed to be boiling over with rage, from questions dying to be answered.

Like a robot, "we must have faith," was spewed towards me; much like a

Mother tells her curious child with the words, "because I say so."

But Selah, what exactly is faith? I tell you after that class my mind changed. My goggles came off and I began to look at the people.

One thing I did learn in that class, is that we are all sinners seeking salvation. But shouldn't there be levels to this thing? Why should a Deacon, Evangelist, and Pastor all be sinners and lead other people? I mean if I come to this place for healing, surely, other sick people cannot heal me, can they? How exactly can I be healed by someone who has the same malady as me?

I am not trying to be cynical but I really wanted the holy spirit, like those women who ran up the aisle or those men who fell when touched.

I needed to know exactly what I was doing wrong. I wanted to be moved, not for show, so that I knew that the GOD that they spoke about, the one given to us, loved me too.

But Selah, GOD never showed up to me like that.

Instead, I watched the sins of the people I met overflow into the aisles and bounce from person to person.

It was as if, the GOD they talked about could not see the maladies as they moved, that blessings only came when praise was performed just right.

I was no longer drunk from the high of a new thing, from wanting to be accepted, but rather, I was afraid.

I listened, watched, and prayed silently for clarity. Sitting right up front, close enough to hear some exchanges during confession time or rather "Altar Call;" I heard that sister tell the Evangelist about her drug addiction, then I saw that same Evangelist, counsel a brother who had tried drugs for the first time at the next gathering. He was overflowing with tears and the Evangelist made no connection, and I would call it a fluke if, I had not heard that man talk to the deacon about his sex addiction, then heard a young woman confessing about having sex for the first time. There were so many other examples; the drunkenness that passed from person to person, the confession of overspending and people praying and coveting things they had never wanted before it seems, all said from the mouths from others who had been "delivered."

While I felt like a violator for listening, I couldn't help for overhearing because I was trying to catch the spirit, and heard them shouting their issues before the body of believers.

I felt like a mad man; seeing the issues, sins, or problems, whatever you wanted to name them, leave one person and bounce onto the next person like a virus.

I had to leave without even catching the spirit.

I felt like a failure.

But not really, because they gave us that religion; and Selah, it felt broken and fragmented. Kind of like a puzzle, missing pieces of the whole. Except members are punished in cycles for going; by sharing in the sins of others unknowingly.

What happened in those walls felt like, what was happening in this community where my skin is seen as a curse. That space cultivates the condition out here. I wanted to be seen by GOD but I cannot even be seen by my people unless I look and act like them without question.

I watched the cycles repeat, and sins pass from person to person so easily. It is a mirror of the streets. They gave us these streets, ghettos, and this GOD but none of it feels right. It feels hollow and empty like it was not meant for us.

Now Selah, tell me how can I go to the altar in there when it produces the same outcome as standing on the street corner out here?

The Exchange

Wow, brother, you said a mouthful. I want to start by saying, I see you. I value you and you do not have to perform any actions for me to acknowledge you.

I think it is brave for you to admit that you never caught the holy spirit. I honor that fact that you did your research and know your history. It takes a strong man to admit, even when you are not sure, that you go back to what is familiar. I want you to consider the fact that when you went in and felt elated that the members called you "full of spirit" yet you still searched for connection the way others received it. Now I will not insult your intelligence to say that we were not given the GOD you found in that body of organized religion. I make no assumptions about what you need or do not need. But what do you really seek? Do you want a connection to the spirit or do you want a connection to people? Because if it is the people you are after, join a social club and you will get the same feeling of newness you found and felt like you lost there.

Yes, people who connect share energy.

Yes, people who get used to the routine, forget how to explain, "the way things are" to new people.

And I must admit, the ritual part feels overwhelming, especially if it is not explained; energy is indeed transferrable so your visual spiritual experience is called "discernment." It allows you to see and feel things that may harm YOUR spirit. If that body is not for you, I encourage you to seek another space. But before you go, make an appointment with the Pastor; I am sure you are not the first person to feel this way. We all need some connection, and you never said you did not believe, you said in multiple ways that you did not understand. We are creatures of habit and you WILL see the same ills in the community in that body, for both are the same people.

So, ask yourself, are you having a religious dilemma or community dilemma? But I can tell you they are usually one and the same. No religion, community nor social space is free from the touch of colonialism, so it all feels like a gift, or curse depending on how you look at it, instead of ownership.

More reading into the history of both are required on your part for you to understand the connection. But until then, let us pray together.

Prayer

MOST HIGH we come before you humbled. We understand that before we can see anything outside of ourselves, we first must acknowledge the eyes, head, the body we look out of. But most of all, may we understand that, no one must accept us; for us to be relevant in this world. May we acknowledge that the value of things like skin, money, social class, and actions are a product of deeply rooted stigmas for which we must overcome if we are to seek your face in earnest. Guide us as we seek answers about the origins of things so that we may worship in truth and honesty. Great IAM you are living, and as we grow to understand the value of our own lives, may we not look at others as a gauge of the rightness of our personal paths. May we never build monuments in our minds of spaces where you can dwell, for we know that all the Earth is your dominion and that the Holy Spirit we seek can be found in rivers, sunrises, and our homes; just as readily as it is found at the front of the body of worshipers. Open our hearts and minds to receive the truth of what being loved by you means. Protect our hearts, and minds as we go on this journey towards seeking you.

Do you agree?

Is there anything you want to add?

Yes, Selah,

Most High, reset my heart to help me have a renewed idea of what is right and acceptable to receive your love. May I not be bound by rules of this world, but guided by the spirit. Speak so that I may hear, and shout when I refuse to listen.

All this we ask, with the GREAT IAM in mind.

Amen

Brother that was beautiful. Do not be afraid to say you do not know or lack understanding. If one person does not answer your question, ask another. If you are serious about your walk, "No" is not an answer you accept. We need the people who question, like you, so that we all get a chance to take a second look at our walk towards the light.

Thank you for being exactly who you are.

"Self-Identity"

Selah you know those people who knock on doors trying to convert others to come to study with them? I liked those people. They were bold and came as a family to tell you about their walk with the MOST HIGH.

That was my first experience at the altar. Except there were no hallelujahs or shouting or running up and down the aisle.

The altar was a body of knowledge, and once you taste what is like to be able to study with a group about GOD, your experience is never the same.

One day when I was a teenager, a group came to my house while we were outside playing. Dirty and hair uncombed, I took the pamphlet offered and asked questions that they answered. I had a voice and they heard me.

When my parents got home, I gave them the little card they left with me, that included a number to call so they could pick me up for service. I am from a conservative household, so I could not go alone, but my sister volunteered to go with me.

Did I mention that the pamphlet had the words, "live forever in paradise on Earth?" That phase was important to me because I wanted to understand just what they thought made this current Earth a paradise, they obviously had not been looking around.

I pulled out my bible to fact check the pamphlet because even as a teenager, I was no sucker. But as I turned the pages, I saw some good articles. I was engaged. So, the next thing I knew, I had my pen out, to answer the questions that were at the end of the sections.

Just like they answered questions for me, I wanted to be able to answer questions too; you know to show them that I was worthy, should I be asked to participate. I mean if lions could lay down with children, like the picture on the pamphlet surely, I could speak with these people who came dressed in suits. Even if I did not get to talk, I wanted to be prepared.

Confident I answered the questions right, I anticipated my weekend. I even went back to look and read a couple of more times, I did not want to be looking crazy by giving the wrong answers. Even though it felt like homework, or studying for a test, it was a test of MY choosing.

As promised, the Family came and picked up my sister and me. We enter a worship space with no windows, there was no holy spirit dancing in the aisle or going up to the front to the altar like we were used to seeing in our home church; the one we went to few times a year.

After the greetings, shaking of hands (they did not hug like the places I was used to but it was just as warm) and then finding our seats, I looked around at honest faces, intent on studying.

I glanced at my neighbors who raised their hands during the discussion and answered questions they too had written down in the pamphlet. There were no people giggling at answers, nor arguing about a position or viewpoint. Everyone was respectable, and "Added on" to the answers of other people. The comfort, made me feel bold enough to raise my hand; and although they knew nothing about me, (my parents were not by my side, I was an outsider) they passed the mic down the aisle towards me.

I felt flush when it reached my hand like my voice would get stuck and abandon me, but it did not. I answered the question and no one followed up or "added on," I heard murmurs of agreement. My chest swelled with pride because I proved, I knew the GOD they were studying, seeking, or building relationship with. I felt like I had prepared myself and was well on the way towards gaining entrance into the paradise they spoke of. The family who brought me congratulated me, and service continued. After the service, they gave me the pamphlet for the next week and dropped us off at home.

I felt like I found where GOD lived. It felt like the great IAM dwelled with those people and they each took a little piece home with them. Being in their midst, I took a piece home too. My sister and I went every week for a month. The way they carried themselves, the peace they had about them, the reminder through weekly study to focus on doing what is right, began to seep over into our lives.

My Father pointed out that we were beginning to get above ourselves and we needed to be brought down to reality. Chores were waiting for us after service, extra things; it felt like a deterrence to keep us from going, but I was willing to make the sacrifice to be able to have paradise on earth.

Then one Sunday, the family picked us up, the father got out and knocked on the door. He stood face to face with our Father and asked if we could come out to eat with their family, in a restaurant. My Father said ok. My sister and I ordered a meal and shared it, we did not want to be greedy. But what I loved about the dinner was that they talked about GOD even though they were not in the worship building.

They said grace together. They chatted about school and life using words that lacked cursing but had emphasis. We drank it in, my sister and I, then we were dropped off at home with big smiles on our faces.

But when we walked in the door, my Father was sitting in the living room and eyed me with pure hatred. He said, how dare I have that family come to him to beg on our behalf. I did not argue, I listened, and as he spoke, the words deflated the excitement I had previously held.

I felt guilty and confused Selah. The people were just being kind to us. My Father endured us going to one more service and then told us we were no longer allowed to go anywhere with "those people."

I had tasted part of paradise on earth and he wanted to snatch it away from me. Being a child, I just shut down. I looked around at our environment, thought about the language used in our home and felt a lack. I concluded that my Father did not want us to go, because we were not good enough to go.

I no longer got those nice neat pamphlets because my Father had called and told them never to come to our house again.

We never saw the family again.

I hid my pamphlets in my room and read my bible when no one was around because it was all I had left of paradise.

When I became an adult, I learned that my Father grew up in that religion, that he had lost his way and they excommunicated him. Once I heard that I decided to give it another try now that no one could tell me no.

And like magic, a member knocked on my door the next week. I was invited out to the service, except I was not given a pamphlet, they explained that they were only reserved for members. So, I got a stapled set of papers to study from; but I was just elated to be studying again.

I did my work. Showed up to service and in this new body, this new city. But what I experienced as a child, did not happen in this space. The outreach team stood up and reported their "field service" progress. They stated that they had went door to door in the "needy" neighborhood as they called it. Then someone snickered and said, "I will bet, not one of those heathens wanted to come" I was shocked and embarrassed. Because I was a heathen from that neighborhood.

I really did lose paradise on earth.

All those feelings as a child came rushing back. My Father was right, I was not good enough to be a member, to dwell here, "in paradise on Earth." I was just another body counted towards their conversion notch.

So, Selah, tell me; how can I go to the altar when I do not fit in there?

The Exchange

I am sorry you experienced that. But sis, think about this, the "paradise on Earth" came through your mind and acceptance. You did the work. You researched, you made a choice to dwell in that body. People are people. But the way you describe your deep dive into understanding what the GREAT IAM is, it is an honorable thing.

You said, that those people got to take GOD home with them after service, and you felt you did too. Do you think you lost the GOD you found because of the actions of your Father or even of the body that introduced you to seek the face of GOD? You were the key ingredient!

Please do not get distracted by the clothes they wore or the things they had. The richness of IAM is not found in those things. Nor do they symbolize paradise on earth as you call it. Let us pray together

The Prayer

Most High we come before you to ask you to clear our past interactions with your people. May life reminds us of our individual value. Help us to see that who you are, is found in the mind of each individual. May we seek your face by studying diligently and not allowing others to determine the goal posts and milestones for finding you. May love cover us and honesty find us in forward progress.

Touch our heart and minds, remind us that we are worthy of love. Not just from people but from YOU, no matter our station in life. It has been said that if we knock, the door shall be opened. Great IAM we are knocking.

Guide us toward the literature, the essence of learning YOU. Remind us when we feel insignificant that we are a part of a whole, only to be complete when we join back with you. May we be forgiving of ourselves and appreciate the gift you gave us in the ability to have an individual thought. Turn our hearts back towards finding you.

Is there anything you would like to add Sis?

No Selah,

May we remember the power of our voice and allow no one to silence us.

Amen

Give me a hug.

You are never alone. If you seek a group to study with, start a bible study circle. Advertise on social media, join ones that exist. You never lost GOD, paradise on Earth exists and you hold the key to returning to it.

"What do I want?"

Do you see what I mean? Three stories that address three ways of seeing GOD that people who really seek and express the MOST HIGH should be aware of.

The first story spoke on the fallacy we have of trying to compare the actions of GOD to our parents.

How often do we do that? I know many people who prefer to confess that GOD is a woman because of the nurturing nature of women. They compare the world picture of goodness, mercy, and forgiveness as the feminine qualities observable in Motherhood. And I do not question their reasoning. I am not in the business of tearing down the idea of GOD for others. Because when you attack a person's GOD you attack who they are including their family lineage of belief and no progress can be made when people feel attacked.

While the MOST HIGH is our creator, we must help people to separate the parents we see from the source that flows through us all. People parent differently, may we not become stigmatized into believing there is a relationship between what we know of parents and what we do not know of GOD to fill in gaps of missing information. That is a dangerous walk if we have poor experiences with those who are supposed to nurture our growth.

The second story spoke on the fear and confusion that happens when people enter a house of worship for the first time.

As we seek the GREAT IAM we will search in many spaces for truth. Some people spend their whole life in one religion, others try whatever "feels" like the MOST HIGH. Again, I force no path down anyone's throat. Upbringing, need for order, and ideas of comfort cause people to choose what is best for THEM. Whichever path they choose, the door should be open for them to gain the understanding needed to make a choice. But not at the expense of depending on pomp and circumstance to get them to settle. Asking questions should always be welcomed in some form or another.

The final story spoke on the fear of not being enough on our own to seek GOD.

This situation is one that worries me the most. Media, Literature, and

Propaganda make people question if they are worthy to receive GOD. They wonder if actions, looks or worldly things keep them out of the grace of the GREAT IAM. God is not a quick fix sold in a bottle to drink for instant glow or acceptance. But in reality, how we see ourselves, how we present ourselves, does determine if "GOD" is offered to us from others. I am not saying it is right, but it has been my experience. May we remember the damage done by words and actions within and around the body of believers. No one has a Monopoly on IAM. Remind people to come as they are, before GOD. Not as a clique, but in practice. A word, a phrase, a look can and does keep people from turning towards the MOST HIGH. Do not act like coming before GOD is a secret club for which only members of your fold are allowed to approach.

Let me make it clear, I do not judge the body any person worships in. People find the GREAT IAM through different routes. But what is important to me is that all routes allow clear access, without the boundaries set by mankind.

Because really who can know the heart of GOD? And if we choose…

What if we get it wrong?

What if our religion is not the right one?

In the end, when we leave our bodies when the truth is before our eyes, it is too late to change our minds.

For me, one universal truth exists, and that is, *"prayer is how we access GOD."*

Think over your life.

Think about the situations that keep you from coming before GOD.

What barriers have you placed up?

Can you, will you release other people from the burden of performing the way you imagine GODLY people should act?

Because, if you are not careful, if you lose your way....

They will take your GOD from you and give you theirs; and their concepts look like yours to the naked eye; on the outside; except, yours, the true IAM has no image, only an essence.

But Moses told you that,

"Thou shalt not make unto thee any graven image or any likeness of anything that is in heaven above, or that is in the Earth beneath, or that is in the water under the earth..."

Why do you think the bible says that?

I am not an expert, I am just a woman seeking the face of the MOST HIGH but some call me a prayer warrior. But I consider myself to be, a reminder of life.

Do not ever forget to pray. A thought is a prayer, an action is a prayer and words spilled out from your mouth filled with emotion or calmness is a PRAYER too.

Pray often, alone or with others.

Your heart is rejuvenated by the hope it brings.

Until next time…
Sending you love
Selah

Also, by

LaShonda C. Henderson

Love and Other Thoughts

(A book of Poems and Love Quotes)

Love and Other Thoughts Journal

(A Journal to help Define individual Love)

Selah~ The Myth of Love Heart Changes

(A Novella)

Selah~ The Myth of Love Life Stories

(A Collection of Short Stories)

Capturing Love's Light

(Poems and Prose)

You can find
LaShonda on Facebook at

www.facebook.com/loveandotherthoughts

On
Instagram at
LoveAuthorLCH

On
The Net at
www.Cshantaypublishing.org